PENELOPE
AND OTHER POEMS

Nihil obstat

~~Arthur J. Scanlan, S. T.~~ D.
Censor Librorum.

Imprimatur

✠ Patrick Cardinal Hayes,
Archbishop, New York.

New York February 28, 1927.

❧ PENELOPE ❧

And Other Poems

BY

SISTER M. MADELEVA
of the Congregation of the Holy Cross

D.A &C.

INTER. FRUCTU

FOLIA

New York ❧ London

D. APPLETON AND COMPANY

Mcmxxvii

To
FRED AND VERN

ACKNOWLEDGMENTS

For permission to reprint many of the poems of this book the author wishes to thank the editors of the *Ave Maria*, the *Annals of Our Lady of Lourdes, The Catholic World, The Commonweal, G. K.'s Weekly*, the *Poetry Review, The Queen's Work, The Saturday Review of Literature*.

CONTENTS

PENELOPE

THE KING'S SECRET

CONTENTS

CONTENTS

FOR CERTAIN GRANDCHILDREN

PENELOPE

PENELOPE

PENELOPE never has raveled as I have raveled;
 She never has fashioned the fabrics that I have
  spun;
And neither her heart nor her lover has traveled as
  mine has traveled
Under the sun.

Her web of delay, deliberate, passionate, splendid,
Was tense with allurement, I doubt not; was wet
  with tears;
But love found it raveled, unfinished—a burial robe
  —and ended
Those piteous years.

My fingers run wildly through warps of bewildering
  wonder,
Or dream over woof of caught silence or sudden song;
They tighten on patterns of laughter or fear that is
  stricken thunder!—
O Love, how long?

Is it naught that I pause in my web as yon suitor
  woos me;

PENELOPE

That I ravel at night with regret the design of day;
That loneliness sickens, grief dazes, and doubt pur-
    sues me
With You away?

With a lifetime of years do I lash myself to You and
    bind You,
Do I dare all the seas of the world without compass
    or star;
Past the lands of Calypso and Circe and Scylla I seek
    You and find You,
Be it never so far!

So I fare on the deific pathway my Love has traveled
As I fashion the web that Penelope could not have
    spun,
And ravel the heavenly robe of delay that she could
    not have raveled
Under the sun.

PENELOPE

IF YOU WOULD HOLD ME

IT is so very strange that, loving me,
  You should ensnare the freedom I find sweet,
  Catch in your cunning will my flying feet.
I will not barter love for liberty;
You cannot break and tame me utterly,
For when your careful conquest is complete
Shall victory be swallowed in defeat.
You hold me only when you set me free.

Because my straight, wild ways are in your power
Do not believe that I surrender them.
Untrammeled love is all I have to give.
If you would keep it, do not pluck the flower;
Leave it, I beg, unbroken on its stem,
Wild with the wind and weather. Let it live!

PENELOPE

PATRINS

YES, I shall leave these patrins as I go:
    Plucked grasses here, a few blown blossoms
        there,
To tell you, though I've gone, how much I care;
To tell you, also, should you want to know,
The way I've taken, my Belovéd, so
That you can find me, find me anywhere.
Be still, my heart! You know he does not dare
To follow dreams; have you no signs to show?

Only the wide, white comfort of the stars,
And strange, lone rest within the arms of dawn,
And Love that binds, and Truth that sets me free.
Why should you fear such infinite prison bars?
The wild and wistful way that I have gone
Leads but to peace. Belovéd, follow me.

ON THIS CONDITION

OH, do I love you? Yes, to be brief and plain.
   But from my window, if the day is clear,
   See that far mountain, lonely and austere,
Flush into gradual wonder, where has lain
Passionless, pallid snow. Almost like pain
Rose-splendid radiance wraps it in beauty sheer
As the sun kisses it—wait, wait, my dear—
And passing, leaves it virgin white again.

When we have reached those heights of calm sur-
   render
Where white integrity and love are one,
Then you may compass me with utter splendor,
Nor shall we need to wish our joy undone;
Then you may kiss me, love, or tense or tender;
Then you may shine on me, being my sun.

THE BLACK KNIGHT

WILL naught but sorrow's dregs your heart
        appease?
      You told or read me that last time you came,
Out of a poem you'd written; even its name
I have forgotten; only you asked the lees
Of life for comfort, bitterer than the seas.
I taste with terror all the innocent shame
You dare; its torture burns me like a flame.
Will nothing satisfy your love but these?

I did not tell you that I found you brave,
Nor bid you wear my colors on your crest.
What secret vigil made you sorrow's slave,
And bound ecstatic anguish to your breast,
What ultimate siege of bitterness you crave
You did not tell me, but I should have guessed.

TRIBUTE

I HAVE known mountains when the day was new
Clothed beyond beauty's self in morning splen-
dor;
Have seen them stand like queens, serene and tender,
Against noon's high tranquillity of blue.
I have watched purple mists and rose-white dew
Cling to them, and the young moon, frail and slender,
Shed on them silver homage of surrender.
I have known this of mountains—and of you.

You are the majesty of all my days,
Set in an aureole of morning light,
Set in my life's high noon; against its night
You will be yet the beauty of my ways.
Ah, let me be the moon, crescent and white,
Shining before you, mute with love and praise!

ULTIMATES

ALTHOUGH you know, you cannot end my quest,
Nor ever, ever compass my desire;
That were to burn me with divinest fire;
That were to fill me with divinest rest,
To lift me, living, to God's living breast.
I should not dare this thing, nor you aspire
To it, who no less passionately require
Love ultimate, possessor and possessed.

You who are everything and are not this,
Be but its dream, its utter, sweet surmise
Which waking makes the more intensely true
With every exquisite, wistful part of you;
My own, the depths of your untroubled eyes,
Your quiet hands, and your most quiet kiss.

PENELOPE

MARGINALIUM

I THINK the story of Shalottt is wrong;
   Oh! not the "four gray walls and four gray
      towers,"
The placid isle and prettiness of flowers,
Nor the sweet incongruity of song.
The river slipping by the summer long,
The lads and lasses, barley fields and bowers,
The listless maid, weaving the livelong hours,
The knight; all these are proper; these belong.

But not youth cursed by love, unwitting how,
Drifting to death upon a senseless tide!
Girl, let your mirror break, your web blow wide;
Nail love's bright flag with life's upon your prow.
Know that you have not ever lived till now.
Who said that love would curse and kill you, lied.

FUTILITY

I HAVE to dress you in your shroud
    (A crude device, by no means new)
   And look on you who are so proud
To worms consigned, to ashes bowed,
To keep my heart from loving you.

I have to call your faults by roll
(Who once had sought to find them few)
To scrutinize your flaws of soul,
Then memorize and cite the whole
To keep myself from wanting you.

And when I painfully have taught
My mind to scorn you and forget,
I look upon the thing I've wrought
So futilely. It comes to naught.
I love you and I want you yet.

PENELOPE

TO ONE PROCRUSTES

"He thinks too much: such men are dangerous."

DO not misunderstand the smile
I send from my Procrustean bed;
It means that in a little while
It shall have done and I be dead.

The bed's dimensions are precise;
One simply must be made to fit;
The methods it employs are nice,
Exact, and there's the end of it.

Once I was stretched to fit its length—
I bear about me yet the scars—
Until I grew to dangerous strength
And was much taller than the stars.

Now, I had grown a head too tall—
The selfsame thing may happen you—
So I am being trimmed, that's all;
It was the obvious thing to do.

The process goes on, day by day,
And I shall never question why;
But when my head is cut away
I think that I may hope to die.

THE KING'S SECRET

THE KING'S SECRET

PSYCHE SPEAKS

THE King's secret is a great secret, and she is so
  little to share it,
   Sweet sister, my Body, so timid and fragile to
   bear it;
For she has a lover—the child!—to think of it only
At first will affright her; will leave her all wistful and
  lovely and lonely.

I shall speak of it to her quite simply, in this wise—O,
  heavenly duty!—
"Little sister, a King comes to seek you, desiring your
  beauty.
With the kiss of His mouth He will kiss you; His
  right arm will enfold you;
With His left He will pillow your head, little bride;
  on His heart He will hold you.

"He will ravish you utterly with the white rapture of
  endless caresses
Till all that you are and possess He inhabits, possesses.
Ah! look in my eyes;—do you know; do you fear to
  discover
Who He is that comes seeking your beauty, this King
  Who is God and your Lover?"

PENELOPE

INVITATION

SO come, Fair;
  At the portal of her house Your little love is
      waiting;

Though somewhere
In her shy, strange heart she fears You, hesitating.

O come now!
For that she is wild she wishes You to woo her;

Though somehow,
For she is a child, she would that You pursue her.

Still come, Sweet;
Into Your arms' wide peace, passionate and tender,

Will come, fleet,
Brave, Your little love, in exquisite surrender.

III

THE BODY SOLILOQUIZES

WHO speaks of bridal bed and nuptial splendor
    Waiting the royal Bridegroom and His
       spouse?
These cannot match the innocent couch I tender
The King Who comes to rest within my house.

O blessed nothingness, whence I am able
To furnish forth my Love this little room;
A little bed, a little chair, a table,
A candle's halo in the shining gloom.

There should be flowers where the King reposes,
With subtle fragrance to beguile His rest;
I place, for bridal lilies, bridal roses,
My white, unfolded self upon His breast.

PENELOPE

SURGE, AMICE

WINTER is in Your heart, You say, and birds
   have flown
  And flowers are withering;
Sweet, may a shy girl bring
To You, her Love, her garden's only own
Darlings from lands where it is always spring?

Three flowers I pluck for You:
This red rose of my lips, warm with the south;
See how it trembles and rests
Upon the hungry kiss of Your uplifted mouth
Against whose drouth
I press,
In mute abandonment beyond caress,
These other two
Pale, passionate, beautiful blossoms of my breasts.

Now is my garden ravaged utterly;
Let be!
Winter is over and gone; a few birds sing
Within Your heart—and in my arms is spring.

THE KING'S SECRET

AS ONE FINDING PEACE

THE secret of the King possesses me
    Unutterably.
     I am a child to sudden woman grown
Who never yet has known
Invasion so imperious, so complete,
Blindly and madly sweet.
I am a bud to sudden blossom blown,
Intoxicate, replete
With fragrance most divinely not its own.
I am dew thirstily drunk up
Out of dawn's lifted cup.
I am my own impotent, daring self, plunged in a sea
Ecstatically!

O God, encompass me!
Be infinitely mine to hold, to bound me;
Absorb, consume, encompass and confound me;
Be in me and beneath me and above me;
O Father, love me, love me!
Tremendously be,
Strong God, my sea.

In ultimate joy upon this Lover's breast
I come to rest.

PENELOPE

Peace, like a song
Envelopes me;
Peace, like the night,
Folds me in conscious, beautiful delight.
Never has human love held me in tranquil thrall,
For not to human love does peace belong.
What if I be for the Lord God a wall,
Beauteous as cedar and as cedar strong;
What if I be a door, and sealed to all save Him,
Cunningly joined, guarded by flashing cherubim?
I am a door, a wall, a tower of passionate strength
Around which multitudinously throng
Wild ecstasies, wild loves, unending blisses,
A God's caresses and a Father's kisses.

Presently let this rapture in profounder rapture cease;
A silver bulwark of wrought silence be,
My Father, since that I am come at length,
Captive and free,
Into Your presence as one finding peace.

THE SWIMMER

AFRAID? Of you, strong proxy lover, you, God's
        sea?
    I give you my small self ecstatically,
To be caught, held, or buffeted; to rest
Heart to your heart, and breast to breathing breast;
To know on arms and cheeks, on brow and lips the
        bliss,
The stinging madness of one infinite kiss;
Daring your most exquisite, sweet alarms
In the safe compass of the everlasting arms.

PENELOPE

TO THE INITIATE

MY kiss upon your brow,
  Subtle and cool and continent,
  Is two parts vow
And two parts sacrament.

But to your lips I press
Only the white flame of desire;
If two parts are caress,
Two parts are cleansing fire.

Because you understand
This word beyond life's weak replies,
Belovéd, take my hand;
Belovéd, close your eyes.

THE KING'S SECRET

APOCALYPSE

MY honest mirror shows me wistful eyes
    That look beyond me, calm, inscrutable, wise,
    Into transcendencies I do not know,
Down ways illuminous that I can not go.

My lips are strange to me; they seem to wear
A quick aloofness from some other where,
As if they wait or cherish some caress
Too secret and divine for me to guess.

I look with quiet wonder at my hands
As one who knows, yet scarcely understands
That they are mine, yet only lent to me,
Waiting some sweet and beautiful destiny.

My ears—I have not caught the hidden word,
Sudden, ineffable, that they have heard;
Nor known how surely and divinely far
My feet have walked on paths familiar.

It is the yearning of my heart they share,
The burning rapture of my soul they dare,
Love's first apocalypse; and rapt and dumb,
They wait the Lover's voice, "I come, I come!"

YOUR NAME

I WAS half fearful lest the envious night,
Coming upon my slumber stealthily,
Should guess the secret of my still delight
And take Your name from me.

Wherefore I would not trust my lips to keep
That Word ineffable, that Word of Love,
But folded it upon my heart to sleep,
Clasping my hands above.

Deliberate, lovely morning found me thus,
Nor sought to leave one shining splendor there,
Only Your name, than sun more glorious,
Than moon and stars more fair.

And then I do not know which sooner came;
Waking, or my hands gently pressed apart,
And on my lips the sweetness for Your name
Uprising from my heart.

It seems almost too beautiful to say,—
I had distrusted night and dreaded dawn,
For O, to seek You at the break of day
And find You gone!—

THE KING'S SECRET

But day has now no wonder matching mine,
Nor subtle night in marvelous silver shod,
Because my heart has held a Word divine,
Has kept the name of God.

PENELOPE

CONCERNING CERTAIN MATTERS OF DRESS

I

QUESTIONS ON A NUN'S HABIT

YOU do not think it is because I do not share
 A woman's subtle weakness for the piquancy of
  dress,
Its swift, sure coquetry, its studied carelessness,
That I wear what I wear?
You do not think it is because I do not dare
Its recklessness?
What do you say
Of wearing one's bridal gown
To town,
To church on Good Friday?
Of wearing one's shroud
Every day, all day,
In the heat and the crowd,
On Easter and Christmas day?
You do not tell me that I have bad taste,
Or none at all, or that I am less than fastidious and
  proud.
Is it because you do not wish to waste
Words upon one whose world in secret you deplore?
You are not sorry for me.

THE KING'S SECRET

You do not think me dressed quite unbecomingly?
(You would give much to be attired so adequately?)
Of all the dozen gowns I ever wore
And have abandoned, orchid and shadow-gray and
       powder-blue,
This is the only one that you need envy me.
—You have not ever cared to find me beautiful before,
Have you?

PENELOPE

II

OF CROWNS

FOR captious fashion and capricious fad
I have but small concern or little care.
Not even to plait a belt for Galahad
Should I have shorn the locks that men thought fair;
But for my Lover Lord, divinely glad
I doff the shining crown that was my hair.

III

JEWELRY

PEARLS such as yours a proud queen quaffed one
    day;
  A jealous queen such diamonds flung away;
Your ring once Portia might have haggled for;
Your bracelets finer are than Esther wore.

A queen brought me my beads from Nazareth,
Egypt and Judah; she was done to death
Almost in fetching them. What bitterness
She bore, from this cross you, perhaps, can guess.

Her only Son was nailed upon it—see,
Jesus of Nazareth, on Calvary;
And this inscription Pilate fastened there.
Beads are the only jewelry I wear.

GOOD OUT OF NAZARETH

GOOD OUT OF NAZARETH

I

MAYTIME

IF Maytime in this golden land
  Is sweet as death,
    How heavenly fair it must have been
In Nazareth!

If flowers here a glory are,
What had they been
Abloom about the feet of her
Who is their Queen!

The little winds that here blow wild,
Grown gentle there,
Adoringly had touched her cheek
And kissed her hair.

And O, if heavens here are blue,
What lovelier skies
Had they beheld, deep mirrored in
Their Lady's eyes!

When Maytime here is loveliest
I catch my breath
To think how fair it must have been
In Nazareth.

PENELOPE

II

THE JUST MAN

I AM with various griefs acquainted well;
   Through tense and tender days at Nazareth
   I walked with anguish bitterer than death,
And doubt less merciful and kind than hell.
There, too, came utter loneliness to dwell,
(My loved one tarrying with Elizabeth).
I have not piteous word nor piteous breath
The bitterness of Bethlehem to tell.

It is not bitterness will break my heart,
But this; a mother's smile, a Babe's weak cry,
A little cheek to stroke, a hand to kiss!
Ah! I could push the stars of heaven apart,
And dare the awe-full face of God most high
For strength to bear such ecstasy as this!

GOOD OUT OF NAZARETH

III

RETURN

O HOLY House of Nazareth,
Your quiet door,
Open to greet your Lord's return,
Need wait no more.

O Mother, leave off listening;
No ear shall tell
Of those returning, wounded feet
You love so well.

He comes, more sudden-sweet than wings
On rapturous quest,
And you are clasped within His arms,
Close to His breast!

PENELOPE

THE YOUNG PRIEST'S MOTHER

YES, he is mine if miracles of weaving
Flesh from my flesh and blood into the fine
Potencies of white manhood, every line
Perfect past mute desire or proud believing
Can make him; if the mystery of achieving
Out of a human son this son divine
Owes aught to motherhood, then he is mine
Beyond my body's gift, my soul's conceiving.

And I am his beyond the extremest guesses
Of men, bound by indissoluble bands
Forever. It is not only he who blesses
And holds me close, but oh! he understands
Why adoration burns in my caresses,
What wounds I kiss upon his beautiful hands.

PROUD BOAST

INCONSTANT Peter, what is this you dread,
This word a servant girl speaks scornfully,
"Surely thou wert with Him in Galilee"?
For shame! Whence has your vaunted courage fled;
Where now is your quick sword, unscabbarded?
What boast, O Simon, could more glorious be;
"Thou art of Christ; thy speech betrayeth thee"?
Damsel, this word of yours has been well said.

I charge you, have the selfsame thing to tell
Of me, when in the outer hall of death
I wait the end, inexorable and grim;
Proclaim then to the councilors of hell,
"This man with Jesus was, of Nazareth;
Even his dying speech betrayeth him."

MY WINDOWS

THESE are my two windows; one
Lets in morning and the sun,
Lets in tranquillity and noon,
Lets in all magic and the moon.

One, looking on my garden, shows
Me miracles: a sudden rose,
A poppy's flame, a tulip's cup,
A lily's chalice lifted up.

Wonder-windows! who could guess
The secret of their loveliness?
Beyond transfigured sky and clod
My two windows show me God.

FANTASY

DO you suppose
     The cherry tree's white furbelows,
     The pretty frills the jonquil shows,
The maple's curious, knotted bows,
The first, pale ruffles of the rose
Are baby things that April sews
For the sweet world to wear?
Who knows?

DESERT SUNSET

SUNSET stood at the edge of the world, apart in
the west,
Virginal, calm, aloof, in golden austerity
dressed.

Soft little twilight winds and birds and clouds had
flown;
Sunset stood on the lone horizon, wistful, alone,

Clad in dispassionate amber from foot to beautiful
head,
Whence all the shining, shimmering glamour of life
had fled.

Almost I thought her a queen, so splendidly simple she
stood;
Almost I thought her a poet in the arms of an elate
mood,

Until I saw the day look down at her from the blue
In vain, and the night look up in vain; then I knew

That virginal, consecrate, lone must sunset forever be,
Taking her mystic way to the heart of eternity.

40

GOOD OUT OF NAZARETH

Aye, and my soul stood there, too, at the utter edge
   of the world,
Plighted, like her, and elate, in golden wonder furled.

PENELOPE

BERNADETTE TAKES
LEAVE OF HER FLOCK

DEARLINGS, my flock, how safe ye be;
How glad ye skip; ye wander free;
Ye sleep so warm and safe. Ah, me!

Shepherdess Mary through the cold
Watched on Bethlehem's wind-swept wold;
One wee Lamb was all her fold.

Dearlings, my lambkins, as ye lave
And quench your thirst at the gracious Gave
Some drink for another Lambkin save.

For Shepherdess Mary—she, so mild—
Fled by night through the desert wild,
Fled with her Lamb that was her Child.

Dearlings, my littlest lamb, and all,
Down on your knees in pity fall;
Here is grief that will your dumb hearts appal.

Shepherdess Mary stood beside
The cross where her Lamb was crucified,
Nor did not die when her one Lamb died,

Nor made no moan, nor did not weep!
She is the shepherdess to whose keep
I give you all, my darling sheep.

42

GOOD OUT OF NAZARETH

She will walk the pastures, unseen of you,
In her kirtle white and her girdle blue,
And a golden rose for each small shoe.

So I leave you, dearlings, but safe ye be;
Glad may ye skip and wander free;
Shepherdess Mary folds you for me.

ANOTHER LOURDES

NO crutches hang before this little shrine,
　　No chant uprises from a movéd throng;
　　But who has touched with strength the cling-
　　　　ing vine?
Whence has that bird its ecstasy of song?

No votive candle at this grotto glows;
No mystic stream with healing fraught is there;
But who has lit the taper of the rose
Or drunk the living font of children's prayer?

Here is no miracle of hidden might;
But who shall speak of bondage and release?
Whence, O my blinded eyes, this sudden light?
Whence, O my waiting heart, this longed-for peace?

GOOD OUT OF NAZARETH

SEAT OF WISDOM

OTHERS before to-day,
    Mary, have hailed you Seat of Wisdom, Grace
        of the Way;
Others have watched the dawn
Break from that desolate darkness that you trod upon,
As in deific promise first they heard
Spoken that word
Transcendent, that a curséd world should feel
Salvation, Woman, through your potent heel.
Kings have, in song elate, ecstatic dream,
Had you for theme;
Prophets have sung
In what array your beauteous flags are flung.
In sheer delight
The sun, eclipsed, glories to find you bright;
And for your crown
Precipitate stars have flung their burning splendor
        down;
The moon beneath your feet
Has set itself for silver pathway, Sweet.
The emulous cherubic hosts might well have striven
For that august evangel unto Gabriel given,
Word consummate
To you, of womankind predestinate.

45

PENELOPE

Beyond all meed desired or dreamed or heard
Elected you God, the Word;
But all the rest might well
Have silence been, desolate more than hell
Save that you said
God's will in you should be accomplishéd.
Hail, Mary, Seat of Wisdom, Grace of the Way!
We greet you as archangels and as children may;
And kneel, your plighted daughters, at your feet,
Waiting your answer meet.

ANTISTROPHE: WISDOM SPEAKS

You wait my word.
What answer shall I give more meet than that she
      heard
Who was to give,
First among women, name to my high prerogative;
My soul doth magnify the Lord, for He
Hath done to me
Things too ineffably beautiful to tell.
For not in Jacob do I dwell;
No, not in Israel nor Salem town
Of high renown.
Ah! come that you may see,
My daughters, where my beauteous dwellings be.
The heavens were not unfurled,
From the beginning and before the world,

46

GOOD OUT OF NAZARETH

Daughters of humankind,
Think that the everlasting God had me in mind.
The poles were not brought forth,
The south's fertility nor the might of the north.
Water was not articulate in any stream or fountain,
Nor earth ambitious was of hill or mountain.
Only with me
Was the sufficient Godhead pleased unutterably.
Eternally within my breast
Wisdom had built her nest,
Until was done
This, that a virgin should conceive and bear a Son.
Content and spaciously has lain within my womb,
The one inn of the world that gave Him room,
Christ; and this chaste and sure retreat
Is Wisdom's holy seat.

EPODE: DEDICATION

What think you of this woman, Mary,
As daily she plies back and forth and up and down
The tasks of home, the errands of the town,
Simple and kind and ordinary
The day long? O, but when night comes to keep
Still vigil, she flies to the arms of God to sleep.
Can this be Wisdom's queen?
Note this to her renown:
She wrought embroidery in the temple, rare;

PENELOPE

She dwelt in Nazareth, obscure, serene;
She fashioned swaddling garments for her Child to
    wear;
She wove the seamless robe that served Him for all
    save shroud;
She heard Him hailed and jeered at by the crowd;
She saw Him done to death.
What wisdom is there here, what consummate art,
What save the pity of a mother's broken heart?
Her ways were silent ways, but when she spoke
Omnipotence manifest within her Son awoke.
Her ways were prudent ways—
Be that remembered in these later days.
Our path is plain to see;
Ah, let us emulous be
Of her who from eternity has been
Wisdom's sole queen.
Mother, within your halls, beneath each spire and
    dome,
Welcome us home.

48

FOR CERTAIN GRAND-CHILDREN

FOR CERTAIN GRANDCHILDREN

THE BISHOP CALLS

FREDERIC is at the door to meet him,
   With James and John in the hall to greet him;
   Mary Lucia, darling thing,
Is on her knees to kiss his ring.

Frederic climbs in the chair beside him;
James and Lucia almost hide him,
Perched at each arm; upon his lap
Sits John enthroned, sweet little chap.

There the four settle themselves sedately
Around the bishop, serene and stately.
The grown-ups gasp in amused dismay;
His Lordship insists that they are to stay.

Perhaps you consider this quite appalling
In children when the bishop is calling,
Because you do not know, I suppose,
The things that a child or a bishop knows.

THE DREAMER

FOR JAMES FRANCIS

I SEE thee, lad, against the painted hill
Lost in such dreams as thou art dream-
  ing still.

Thy brothers all apparel have more sober
Than thine, October,

Nor boasts in all his glory Solomon
The coat of many colors thou hast on.

FOR CERTAIN GRANDCHILDREN

THE GAME

DEAR little girl, thou art playing;
  What may thy sweet game be?
  A mighty realm thou art swaying,
Lady of high degree,
With royal hosts obeying,
And the Lord Sovereign paying
Thee gentle fealty.
I see;
Dear little girl, thou art praying;
All heaven waits on thee.

TO SWING YOU

YOU want me to swing you way up high,
  Up through the branches, up to the sky,
  Higher and higher yet, until
You catch your breath and your heart stands still;

And I watch you, lovely flying thing,
A sweet, bright bird of a child on wing,
With eyes all shining and lips apart!
On a sudden I catch you to my heart;

There, little girl, I can swing you far
Past the topmost branch, past the day-quenched star
To that heaven away beyond the sky;
I can swing you as high as my love is high.

FOR CERTAIN GRANDCHILDREN

TO A YOUNG GIRL

SWEET girl, adieu—
Word literally true—
It is to God that I relinquish you.
The gate of your white life, apocalyptic pearl,
Swings quickly to
And you have passed from me into God's keeping.
Already in this first immortal hour
Your young years, which like petals did upcurl
In promise exquisite, unfold, unfurl
To perfect, heaven-blown, and forever fadeless flower,
Your lovely blossomed self.   O, child, why am I
    weeping?
God saw you ripe to sudden fruit, to this swift reaping.
Adieu, sweet girl.

STARS

WE are the stars that have watched the night
skies with the prophets of old;
We are the Magi from out of the East; we
are bringers of gold.

Heaven has incense of praise from censers seraphic to
bring;
Earth, the world-weary, bears bitter-sweet treasure of
myrrh to the King.

Homage of incense and myrrh for a God and a Saviour
are meet;
We are your stars, little King, and we scatter the gold
of ourselves at Your feet.

FOR CERTAIN GRANDCHILDREN

AT SHADOW TIME

I WATCH the shadow folk creep down,
The white-faced stars climb up the sky:
I hear the little winds go by:
I see the far lights of the town.

I feel that peace is over them
And out of it this word I hear,
"The blessed time is very near,
The holy night at Bethlehem."

Over and over I repeat,
"O Bethlehem, O holy night,
O angel host, O starry light
Above a Baby small and sweet."

Then how I wish that I had been
A holy king, a shepherd dumb;
With what glad haste I would have come
To see the things that they have seen!

Scarce do I wish when lo! I see
A Lady in God's beauty dressed,
A sleeping Babe upon her breast,
Walk past me very quietly.

PENELOPE

I think she comes a far, far way;
I think she walks the wide world's gloom,
Seeking somewhere a little room
In which her precious Child to lay.

But now her eyes grow large and bright;
I see that she has found a place,
And from the smile upon her face
The darkness blossoms into light.

"Here is a place, my little One,"
She whispers low, "where You may bide;
And room there is for me, beside;
A place of love it is, my Son.

"A place kept but for You alone;
And look You, what a beauteous thing,
Here You will reign, my little King,
Where love has built for You a throne."

Gently she lays her Babe to rest
In this place holy and apart;
The place I know; it is your heart
That loves this Child and loves Him best.

Then once again do I repeat,
"O Bethlehem, O holy night,

FOR CERTAIN GRANDCHILDREN

O angel host, O starry light
Above a Baby small and sweet."

I watch the shadows fall and hear
The little winds; I take your hand
In mine and we both understand
That Bethlehem is very near.

(1)

THE END